# UPDATE:

# Drinking and Driving

by Deborah Crisfield

CRESTWOOD HOUSE
Parsippany, New Jersey

Cartoon drawings by Jim Kirschman

## PHOTO CREDITS

Cover: courtesy of Mothers Against Drunk Driving
Courtesy of National Highway Traffic Safety Administration: 6, 12, 20
Courtesy of Mothers Against Drunk Driving: 17
Brian Vaughan: 33
Courtesy of Students Against Drunk Driving: 36, 43

Published by Crestwood House, an imprint of Silver Burdett Press.
A Simon & Schuster Company
299 Jefferson Road, Parsippany, NJ 07054

First edition
Printed in the United States of America

10 9 8 7 6 5 4 3 2 1

Library of Congress Cataloging-in-Publication Data

Crisfield, Deborah.
    Drinking and driving / by Deborah Crisfield — 1st ed.
        p.    cm. — (Update)
        Includes bibliographical references and index.
        ISBN 0-89686-810-9
        1. Drunk driving—United States.  2. Drunk driving—United States—
Prevention.  3. Drunk driving—United States—Prevention—
Citizen participation.  I. Title.  II. Series: Update.
    HE5620.D7C77    1995
    363.12'51—dc20                                                    94-3647
        Summary: Discusses the problem of drinking and driving in the United
States with an emphasis on what young people can do to prevent drunk
driving. Includes a listing of organizations that aim to stop drunk driving.

# Contents

# DRINKING AND DRIVING

# FIRST TIME?

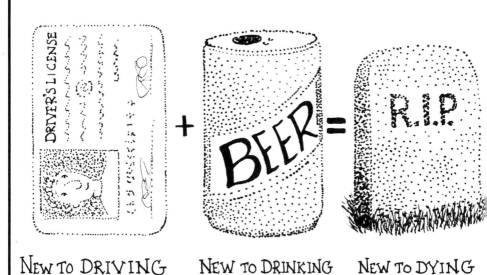

NEW TO DRIVING       NEW TO DRINKING       NEW TO DYING

# Driving While Intoxicated (DWI)

The University of New Hampshire fraternity party was winding down as six students headed out into the cold February air to cap off the night with a pizza. "I'll drive," said Larry Evans. "I've only had a few drinks."

The group piled into Larry's small Toyota. Two people had to sit on laps, but no one minded. The pizza place was just across town. Besides, no one but Larry wanted to risk driving drunk.

But Larry was beginning to wonder if he should really be driving. Maybe he'd had more to drink than he remembered, because he just couldn't seem to steer the car straight. He tried to concentrate, but it was no use with all the horseplay in the backseat.

"Keep it down, okay?" he turned around and yelled.

"Look out!" someone screamed.

## Did You Know...?

• One DWI-related injury occurs every ninety seconds in the United States.

• Some insurance companies have clauses in their contracts that allow them to get out of paying a driver who caused a DWI accident. In fact, all drivers in Maryland have this clause in their policies!

• At current rates, 40 percent of Americans will be involved in a DWI situation at some point in their lives—as a driver or as a victim.

• One regular-size beer (12 ounces) has the same effect as one average glass of wine (8 ounces) or one mixed drink (1.5 ounces of alcohol).

**Drinking and driving is a dangerous, often deadly mix.**

Larry whipped his head back, but it felt as if it were moving in slow motion. They were heading off the road. Slamming on the brakes, Larry jerked the steering wheel to the left. The car skidded straight toward the edge of the road. Larry couldn't remember what to do. He turned the wheel back to the right, but it was too late. The car crashed through the guardrail. The two passengers sitting on laps died in the hospital the next day. Larry came out of the crash with a ruined car, broken ribs, a load of guilt, and a lawsuit.

This tragic 1990 crash was a direct result of DWI. **DWI** stands for **driving while intoxicated. Intoxicated** is another word for drunk. The term **DUI** is also used. This expression stands for **driving under the influence**—under the influence of drugs or alcohol. These terms are used interchangeably. DWI or DUI is illegal in all 50 states.

Alcohol slows a person's reflexes, judgment, and perception. All of these are needed to drive a car safely. It's not surprising, therefore, that almost half of all car crashes in this country are alcohol-related.

When drinking is mixed with driving, the car changes from being one of the great conveniences of modern life into being a dangerous and deadly weapon. In fact, according to the National Highway Traffic Safety Administration (NHTSA), four times as many Americans died in drunk- driving crashes in this decade than were killed during the Vietnam War, the nation's longest war, in which 58,000 Americans died.

## Accident or Car Crash?
Activists working to put a dent in drunk-driving deaths never refer to DWI crashes as accidents. Accidents are random and unavoidable, but DWI crashes can be prevented if people make responsible decisions.

Drinking and driving involves two major decisions: the decision to drink and the decision to drive. If you choose to drink and then drive, you are running the risk of crashing your car. If your car crashes, it's no accident.

"I talk to a lot of convicted drunk drivers in a program to show them the damage they have done to innocent people," says Paula Moore, a paralyzed 37-year-old victim of DWI. "And they all say the same thing: 'I'm sorry. It was an accident. I never meant for it to happen.'

"Well, I just don't buy that. Of course they didn't want to be in a car crash, but somewhere along the line they made a conscious decision not to worry about the consequences of their actions."

## Drunk-Driver Profile

One-fifth of all drivers admit to having driven under the influence, and there are probably many more people who won't admit it or don't realize it. Drunk drivers come from both sexes, all races, all ages, and all levels of the economic scale. But in the battle to fight drunk driving, we need to know who is most likely to cause a DWI crash and why. Only then can steps be taken toward change.

The typical drunk driver who dies in a DWI crash is a male under 30 who doesn't like wearing a seat belt. He's had a lot to drink, and the odds are he's been stopped for drinking and driving at least one other time. Here are the statistics:

1. According to a 1991 NHTSA report, males who die in car crashes are twice as likely as females to be drunk.

2. The same study divides age groups into five-year blocks, and the young do not come out ahead. Of the 12 divisions, the 16–20 age group had the most fatal car crashes (7,989). The 25–29 age group had the most DWI fatal car crashes (2,479 out of 7,418), and the 21–24 age group had the highest percentage

of DWI fatal car crashes (2,272 out of 6,738, or 33.7 percent). Compare that with the 50-54-year-olds who had only 368 fatal DWI crashes out of 2,351 total crashes.

3. The NHTSA also reports that only 14 percent of drunk drivers who were killed in crashes were wearing seat belts.

4. Over half the people arrested for DWI had the equivalent of 12 beers before getting behind the wheel. And almost one-third of the people had the equivalent of 22 beers!

5. In a 1992 Bureau of Justice Statistics study, more than half the people jailed for DWI in 1989 had previous DWI convictions. About 1 in 6 had at least three other jail terms for drunk driving!

Many people assume that all drunk drivers are alcoholics. This is not true, although alcoholics certainly make up a fair share of drunk-driving arrests. According to a study written up in *Fortune* magazine, an alcoholic is less likely to be arrested for DWI than a reckless youth. Alcoholics tend to be cautious. They may be experienced at hiding their drinking and therefore are extra careful behind the wheel.

## Blood Alcohol Content

Lawmakers needed a way to measure how drunk a person is. They decided to measure drivers' blood alcohol content, or the BAC. The BAC compares the amount of alcohol in the bloodstream with the total amount of blood. The comparison is important because people differ in size. A woman who weighs only 100 pounds will be far more affected by one drink than a man who weighs 220 pounds.

In most states, drivers with BAC levels of 0.10 or more are considered to be DWI. But newer studies have shown that even lower BAC levels can cause problems. The Insurance Institute for Highway Safety (IIHS) has found that a BAC as low as 0.02 can affect driving ability. The same study indicates that the probability of a crash increases after a BAC of 0.05 and jumps up an enormous amount after 0.08.

Because of these new findings, eleven states have already lowered the legal BAC to 0.08, and many other states have bills stalled in the legislature. It's tough to get the bills passed because many people accept alcohol as a significant part of their lives. Afraid that it will be bad for business, restaurant and bar owners are fighting the new limit, too.

The difference between an 0.08 BAC and a 0.10 BAC is about one drink over two hours. For instance, a 130-pound woman could have four drinks in two hours and have a BAC lower than 0.10. If she wanted her BAC to be lower than 0.08, she would have to limit herself to only three drinks in two hours. A 165-pound man could have five drinks to be under 0.10, and four drinks to be under 0.08.

The BAC is very easy to measure, and no blood has to be drawn. A device called a **breathalyzer** can measure the amount of alcohol in a person's body just by examining the person's breath. In New Jersey, a person who refuses to take a breathalyzer test loses his or her driver's license automatically for six months!

## The Arrest

Police look for a number of clues to identify drunk drivers. Richard Asarnow, a police officer in Summit, New Jersey, lists a few. "We watch for drivers who can't stay in their lanes and who turn their high beams on and off a lot as if they can't see well. Drunk drivers tend not to use their turn signals, and they're often impatient, honking their horn. Frequently, we identify them by their speed changes, going fast, slowing down, going fast again. But the majority of drunk drivers we find at the scene of an accident."

After stopping the car, the officer puts the driver through some **standardized field sobriety tests.** These tests require balance, coordination, and clear thinking and are harder for a person who is drunk. Drunk drivers may have difficulty doing these tasks:

1. Walk in a straight line, touching heel to toe.
2. Raise one leg and balance on the other while counting out loud.
3. Move the eyes from side to side, following a stimulus, without involuntary eye jerking.

If the driver fails these tests, the police will make an arrest and take the driver to the police station. There the officers give the driver a Breathalyzer test and may repeat the standardized field sobriety tests in front of a video camera.

A suspected offender performs a standardized field
sobriety test for police.

"The videotapes are useful for when we have to appear in
court," says Officer Asarnow. "Sometimes a driver will be
protesting that he wasn't drunk, but once he sees how he
was acting on the video, he'll agree. People don't realize just
how seriously drinking affects them."

## DWI Laws

After a driver is arrested, he or she will
be given a court date. At court a judge will listen to the
facts, hear the police report, and see the videotape, if available. The judge will also hear about the arrested person's
driving history, such as whether the person has ever been
arrested for DWI before. Once all the testimony has been

given, including the driver's defense, the judge will decide if the driver is guilty. If the driver gets a guilty verdict, the judge will also tell the driver his or her sentence. Sentences may involve jail, fines, **community service**, driver education courses, and **license suspension** or **license revocation**. Any combination of these is a possibility.

Some states have mandatory sentences for DWI convictions. The judge has a time range, such as jail for 30-60 days, but he or she must give the convicted driver at least the minimum of 30 days. The same is true of fines, which range from $100 to $5,000 throughout the country.

Seventeen states have mandatory license suspension for DWI. That means that convicted drunk drivers are not allowed to drive for a certain amount of time. But at the end of that period, the person gets his or her license back.

Eight states hit a little harder. They have mandatory license revocation. If a license is revoked, the offender, like a new driver, must apply for a license all over again once the revocation term is up.

Until the mid 1980s, drunk-driving laws and enforcement were fairly lenient. People would reason, "I won't get caught, and even if I do, I'll just have to take a few classes. It's worth the risk." Fortunately, the DWI laws in most states have gotten a lot tougher. On top of that, insurance is incredibly expensive for a person who has had a DWI arrest. Now people are forced to stop and think, "Maybe I will get caught, and I'll lose my license, go to jail, or owe a lot of money. Maybe it's not worth it."

# NEW WAYS TO FIGHT DWI

# Good News and Bad

In 1992 over 39,000 people died in traffic accidents. Almost half of the deaths (17,700, or 45.1 percent) occurred in alcohol-related crashes. That averages out to about 1 alcohol-related death every 30 minutes.

That's the bad news. The good news is that the number keeps getting smaller every year. Back in 1982, for instance, there were 43,945 traffic accidents, and alcohol-related crashes accounted for 25,165 of them. That's 57.2 percent!

The reduction hasn't been easy. New strategies are always being developed, and there's still a long way to go. But the efforts by government and private citizens have already made a difference.

## Administrative License Revocation

One of the most effective new programs is called **administrative**

---

### Did You Know...?

• An incredible 89 percent of adults favor automatically taking away a driver's license from anyone convicted of DWI.

• About 79 percent of people surveyed in a Harris opinion poll said they would like to see more police checkpoints to catch drunk drivers.

• The Good News
The 15-19-year-old age group beats all the other ages when it comes to reducing DWI deaths. Take a look at the numbers. In 1982 the number of people in this age group who were killed in DWI accidents was 4,133, while in 1992 it was only 1,833.

---

**license revocation (ALR).** In states with ALR laws, arresting police officers can take away a drunk driver's license at the scene of the crash. This stops dangerous drivers from getting back on the road and becomes an inconvenience to people who feel they need to drive. Some offenders still drive illegally without a license, but ALR helps because the offenders are likely to be extra cautious so they won't get caught.

ALR is especially effective with young offenders. Being sentenced to attend more driving classes doesn't seem to help—after all, the original classes are still fresh in their minds. But the threat of losing a newly won license is a powerful incentive to be sober on the road.

The states that have adopted ALR have the statistics to prove that it works. For instance, in North Dakota, drunk- driving deaths went down 37 percent in one year after ALR was passed. In Nevada they went down 41 percent in two years.

## Sobriety Checkpoints

Another effective program consists of police **sobriety checkpoints**. Police set up cones in driving lanes to stop drivers as they pass through. They check to see if the drivers act or smell as if they've been drinking. Every suspected impaired driver is put through the field sobriety tests. The police often have a van nearby with a Breathalyzer, so they can tell right on the spot if someone has been drinking.

Like ALR, checkpoints have made a significant difference in alcohol-related crashes. Even if only a few drunk drivers are caught at the checkpoints, the fear of getting caught is enough to stop many people from drinking and driving. Besides, police at the checkpoint can remind drivers to use their seat belts, which may save their lives down the road.

Most people are in favor of checkpoints. Towns with checkpoint programs have seen big drops in the number of alcohol-related deaths. But a lot of people oppose checkpoints. One complaint is that they cause traffic jams; cars may have to wait in line for up to 15 minutes.

Other people feel that checkpoints violate their rights. They claim that they shouldn't be stopped and examined unless they've done something wrong. Fans of the checkpoints say that the checkpoints are like the security systems at airports. They are in place to protect the rights of innocent

**In some towns, police set up sobriety checkpoints. They stop cars to see if the drivers have been drinking.**

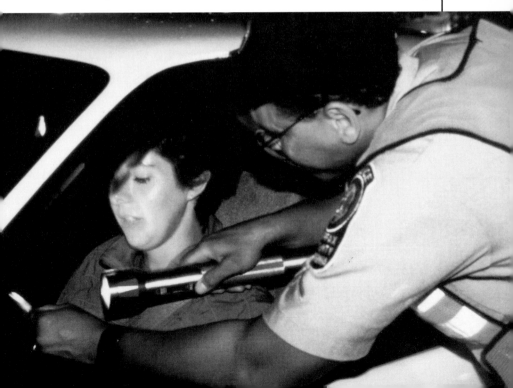

people following the same route as others whose actions might cause severe injury or death. The argument was brought to the United States Supreme Court, which, on June 14, 1990, ruled in favor of the checkpoints.

The courts did say, however, that law enforcement officials must warn motorists that a checkpoint is going to be set up. This frustrates law enforcement because warnings help drinkers avoid the checkpoint and the drunk drivers could potentially be in a crash and kill an innocent person.

Supporters argue that the warning alone has a good effect. A driver who avoids a roadblock on purpose, will probably drive more safely, knowing that police are on the lookout for reckless or drunk drivers.

The cost of sobriety checkpoints is another concern. Each checkpoint requires a number of officers, which means that other officers have to be available to attend to regular police duties. But if the checkpoints result in more arrests, fewer deaths, and more fines, they could pay for themselves.

The bottom line is that checkpoints do reduce drunk-driving deaths. Communities that have used checkpoints have reduced their alcohol-related fatalities by 10 percent.

**Designated Drivers**    One program aimed at stopping drunk driving before it starts is the **designated driver** program. Before people go out for the night, they choose one person to be the driver for the group. That person does not drink alcohol that evening. The next time the group goes out, someone else becomes the designated driver.

# Another Type of Car Key

Scientists and lawmakers alike have been working on methods to bring DWI sensors to cars. Some are in existence already. In a few states, DWI offenders are allowed to choose between going to jail or buying an expensive device, similar to the Breathalyzer, for their car. The device is part of a special lock that attaches to the ignition. The driver must breathe into the device before starting the car. If the device doesn't detect any alcohol, it releases the lock, and the driver can go. This way, the person can never drive drunk!

According to an article in BusinessWeek, a Tokyo University professor is working on a similar invention. This new machine would measure the alcohol in a person's perspiration. If the professor can perfect the device, it will cost a lot less than the devices currently available. Who knows? Maybe one day, alcohol testers will be as standard as seat belts in all new cars.

A police officer operating a Breathalyzer. In a few states, DWI offenders have the choice of going to jail or installing a device similar to a Breathalyzer in their car.

The key to the success of this program is to choose the driver at the beginning of the evening. People often assume that a friend is staying sober, but at the end of the evening, no one is fit to drive. Then the group chooses the least-drunk person to drive, and everybody risks injury. By naming a designated driver in advance, everyone is assured a safe ride home when the night is over.

Many bars and clubs promote the designated-driver program by offering free sodas and other nonalcoholic beverages to the driver. They don't want to be sued if one of their customers gets into an accident.

## Victim Impact Panels

If, despite all these new measures, a person is arrested for DWI, he or she may face a **victim impact panel**—a group of people hurt in alcohol-related crashes who meet with drivers who have caused similar crashes. The first victim impact panel was introduced in 1982 in Rutland, Massachusetts. Now a number of states use them.

Believe it or not, more than half the people jailed for DWI have prior convictions for drunk driving. The fines and the sentences do not always have the impact that they should. They don't convince everyone not to commit the same crime again. The idea behind the victim impact panels is to try something different, to appeal to emotions. That approach may reach some drivers who wouldn't otherwise pay attention.

The victims don't yell at the DWI offenders. Nor do they blame them for anything. Instead, they calmly tell their own stories. They discuss the sorrow they felt when a family member died, or they talk about what it's like to be paralyzed for life. The idea is to force the DWI offenders to see actual victims. This method is more convincing than just reading a bunch of statistics.

# MOTHERS FIGHT BACK

## ALL DRUNK DRIVERS WEAR THE SAME DISGUISE

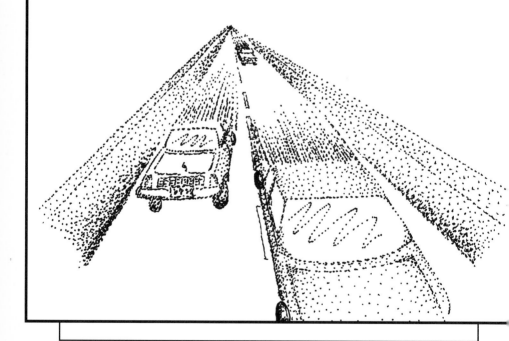

# Mothers Against Drunk Driving

In 1980, a 13-year-old California girl was killed in a drunk driving crash. The man who hit her had been released from jail just two days before, after serving time for another drunk-driving crash. And he had had three other drunk driving arrests!

The girl's mother, a woman named Candy Lightner, was furious that this man had been allowed back on the road. At least, she thought, he would now be put in jail for a long time, so he wouldn't end up killing anyone else.

She was wrong. Nobody was cracking down on drunk driving. The laws weren't very strict. Here was a man who had killed her daughter because of his drinking, had been in another crash because of his drinking, and had three other arrests, yet the judge sentenced him to only two years in

## Did You Know...?

• Since MADD has been in existence, the number of drunk drivers killed in car crashes has dropped more than 40 percent.

• No Bankruptcy
MADD is now trying to push a bill through that would prevent convicted drunk drivers from declaring bankruptcy to avoid paying damages to their victims.

• Car crashes kill more children than any other cause of death. Almost half of these crashes are alcohol-related. It's no wonder that mothers are getting involved!

Jill Bognar will never celebrate the Fourth of July again. Five years ago, she and her husband took their three children to a fireworks show at a local park. The older children were having a great time, but 3-year-old Jessica was afraid of the noise. Jill's husband offered to take Jessica home and let the others stay.

They left, and Jill and the two boys watched the show. The fireworks were amazing, but Jill remembers hearing police sirens and ambulances throughout much of the show. "I just assumed it was another kid who'd hurt himself setting off firecrackers," she recalls.

But when Jill and her sons returned home, she learned the real reason for the sirens. A police officer was waiting in front of the house. He'd gotten their address from her husband's wallet. Jill's husband and her daughter had been killed by a drunk driver on their walk home from the park.

"At first I thought my life was over," Jill remembers. "I couldn't go on without the two of them. I blamed myself. Why did I let them go home? Why wasn't I the one to leave?"

"Later I got in touch with MADD. They helped me shift the blame to the drunk driver. They helped me get on with my life, for my sake and the sake of my sons. I'll never get over this, but I can manage to cope each day with the support of friends I've met through MADD."

prison! And he was able to spend his two years at a work camp and a halfway house.

Candy Lightner knew that something had to be done. If drunk drivers weren't forced to pay for their crimes, there would never be any reason for them to stop drinking and driving. If they weren't put in prison after a drunk-driving crash, then they would be out on the road again, putting someone else's life in danger. So Candy Lightner created a group called Mothers Against Drunk Driving (MADD).

The group's goal was to make the country aware that drunk driving is a crime. MADD set out to **lobby** for tougher laws and longer sentences. It started with a chapter in California and one in Maryland; now it has millions of volunteers and over 400 chapters around the United States and in Canada, England, New Zealand, and Australia.

And MADD's crusade against DWI has worked. Since the group was formed, drunk-driving deaths have dropped nearly thirty percent. MADD has made the public aware of the dangers and tragedies that accompany drinking and driving. The group has been a major force behind raising the drinking age to 21 around the country, lowering the BAC to 0.08, and instituting ALR laws. So far, MADD has helped convince legislators to pass more than 1,400 new drunk-driving laws!

## MADD's Philosophy

Mothers Against Drunk Driving exists for a couple of reasons. The group provides support to people who, in a crash with a drunk driver, have been hurt or who have lost someone they love. MADD also works toward ending drunk driving in the first place.

MADD wants people to know that it is not on a crusade against drinking. The group just wants people to stop combining drinking and driving. It's true that Americans are less likely to drink and drive than they were a decade ago. But still, a major problem exists if 17,699 people died last year because of drinking and driving.

Ideally, MADD would like to see DWI stop completely, but the group has to be more realistic. Solving the problem will take time. Keeping that in mind, MADD's next goal is the **20 x 2000 program**. This program's aim is to reduce DWI-related deaths by 20 percent by the year 2000.

Getting the shocking statistics out to the public and changing the laws covering drunk driving are the two main ways that MADD hopes to achieve this goal. It wants to see ALR in every state. If a driver is caught DWI again, MADD wants his or her vehicle taken away. The group wants jail sentences and fines to be required in every state, even for first offenders. One bill the group is supporting would require even stiffer penalties for someone who is caught DWI with children in the car.

## Lobbying the Government
Since MADD began its work, drunk driving has dropped dramatically—largely because of tougher laws passed by city, state, and national governments. It was partly through MADD's

efforts that these bills were introduced.

Liquor companies, beer distributors, restaurant and bar owners, and many other powerful groups all had a stake in keeping the DWI laws lenient. The average citizen didn't have much clout against these influential organizations; each citizen was just one tiny voice against a massive group.

With the establishment of MADD, the tiny voices banded together to become a powerful force. Once the government knew that many citizens felt the same way, the government tried to pass laws to make those people happy. And when their representatives in government didn't pass the laws they wanted, MADD and its supporters voted for new legislators who would listen to their concerns.

Here are some of the laws that MADD has helped to pass:

1. Minimum drinking age raised to 21 in all 50 states
2. Mandatory, rather than optional, jail sentences and fines in certain states
3. Automatic suspension of the driver's license in some states
4. Victim impact panels used for rehabilitation
5. "Happy hour"—drink specials or free food to attract people to a bar after work—outlawed in certain states
6. Victims of drunk-driving crashes given the same rights as victims of other violent crimes
7. Sobriety checkpoints in certain towns
8. Permission given to victims to sue for damages from bar owners and party hosts who let drunk drivers get behind the wheel of a car

# Public Relations

MADD also hopes to cut down on DWI crashes by creating programs to make people aware of MADD's message. The group has run campaigns all over the country to encourage people to be involved and concerned. For instance, in 1984 MADD set up a writing and poster contest in the schools. Students wrote essays or drew pictures that called attention to the dangers of drunk driving. That year only 2,000 students participated. But in 1990 the number had grown to more than 50,000!

MADD also operates programs like Project Red Ribbon, in which drivers pledge not to drink and drive during holidays. Drivers wear red ribbons to show their support for this program and to remind other people to do the same. This project was started in 1986, and that year MADD passed out 1 million red ribbons!

# Victim Support

MADD's other function is to offer support to the victims of DWI crashes. These people may be the survivors of a crash or families and friends who have lost loved ones to DWI. They may be dealing with their own injuries or the grief of mourning. MADD reaches out to them in several ways.

First, MADD runs a hotline. If a family member is killed or hurt in a drunk-driving crash, many survivors don't know where to turn. But if they call 1-800-GET-MADD, MADD can help them. The hotline is available to everyone, whether they live near a MADD chapter or not. The hotline

# Unhappy Holidays

Holidays are especially bad times to be driving. People are celebrating, and at celebrations there is often a lot of alcohol. Here are some of the 1992 holiday statistics compiled by MADD.

| Holiday | Number of deaths | Number DWI related | Percentage |
|---|---|---|---|
| New Year's | 118 | 89 | 74.8 |
| Memorial Day | 422 | 253 | 55.8 |
| 4th of July | 350 | 196 | 55.9 |
| Labor Day | 446 | 237 | 53.2 |
| Thanksgiving | 399 | 225 | 55.9 |
| Christmas | 391 | 194 | 49.5 |

staff gives the victims support and understanding. MADD's staff tells them what their rights are, gives them tips on finding a lawyer, and offers assistance all through the court proceedings.

MADD can also help victims get in touch with others who have had similar experiences. Sometimes groups of victims get together in support groups. Knowing that they're not alone can be a great comfort. It also helps to know how other people have handled their injuries or sadness. MADD support groups participate in candlelight vigils every year to let people know the pain they have suffered as a result of drunk drivers.

# THE YOUTH MOVEMENT

# Minimum Drinking Age

"I'm old enough to vote, to drive, and to sign my own permission slips. Why can't I drink?" asks an 18-year-old high-school senior.

"Yeah," his friend chimes in. "The government thinks I'm old enough and responsible enough to have a gun in my hand, but I'm too young to have a beer."

The Minimum Drinking Age Law, a national law passed in 1984, is controversial. More than one-third of the voters still oppose it, arguing that once a person is an adult, he or she has the right to be treated like an adult in every situation.

But lawmakers feel that one person's rights stop when they interfere with another person's rights. The excessive drinking and driving done by young people endangers the lives of innocent people. So the 18- to 20-year-old group lost their right to drink because it interfered with the rights of sober people to live safely.

"But why does it have to be everyone? Why can't it be just the offenders?" gripes a 19-year-old. "Why should I

## Did You Know...?

• One third of college students admit to driving drunk on a regular basis.

• Car Raffle
One of the suggestions SADD makes for getting students to stay all night at a school-sponsored, alcohol-free graduation party is to raffle off a donated car. In order to win it, the student must be present at the party. What a great incentive!

• Of all the DWI and DUI arrests in this country, over one-quarter of them are of people under age 25.

have to be punished for what others my age might do?"

It's a fair question, but no one wants to wait until teenagers lose their lives or injure innocent people before cracking down. And no one can argue with the results of the law. Nearly 6,000 lives have been saved because of it!

## Reckless Youth

Since 1982 the DWI deaths of people between the ages of 16 and 20 dropped 44 percent. That's a wonderful statistic, but over 7,000 young drivers still die every year as a result of drinking and driving. In fact, alcohol-related car crashes are the number one killer of people between the ages of 15 and 24.

Other factors, in addition to alcohol, play a role in the large number of underage DWI deaths. For one, people under 30 are the least likely to use seat belts. This is especially unfortunate because these less-experienced drivers need the protection of seat belts.

The inexperience of young drivers contributes to teenage car crashes in other ways, too. New drivers don't know that a car at high speeds, going around a sharp curve, may not be able to grip the road. They don't know how slippery a road can get when it's raining, and they may not know how to steer out of a skid.

On top of these dangers, young people find it hard to believe they will ever die. Many young drivers treat their cars like new toys. They view them as something to play with, rather than as something to make life easier. They race their cars and take them up to high speeds, because, as with other playthings, they want to see what these new toys can do.

When alcohol is combined with inexperience, it's not sur-

A group of young people outside a popular club in New York City. Many teenagers feel that the minimum drinking age of 21 is unfair.

prising that crashes occur. The brain isn't working fast enough to react, and the driving skills are too new to be automatic.

As Jim Arena, the director of New Jersey's Division of Highway Traffic Safety, says, "When you have an inexperienced driver and an inexperienced drinker, you end up with a deadly mix." He's right. In 1991 over 8,000 drunk teenagers caused the death of over 9,000 people, many of whom were the teenagers themselves.

## Students Against Driving Drunk

In 1981 two high school students in Wayland, Massachusetts, were killed because they were driving drunk. The community was devastated. The boys' hockey coach, Robert Anastas, decided that something had to be done. Too many students were risking their lives by drinking and driving. He couldn't let another tragedy like this one ever happen again.

Anastas formed a group called SADD—Students Against Driving Drunk. Wayland High School students got together to learn about the dangers of drinking and driving and to pledge not to do it. The SADD philosophy is that students have to rely on themselves to solve this problem. They have to come to their own conclusion that they don't want to die because of alcohol and that they don't want to bury friends who have died because of it.

Over the years, SADD has expanded its program. It motivates students to do more than just refrain from drinking and driving. Now SADD works to keep students from drinking at all. The organization has created programs that encourage schools to hold alcohol-free proms and graduation parties.

SADD's efforts have met with great success. Schools all

over the country are adopting their methods, and DWI deaths have dropped enormously.  In 1981, before SADD's programs were adopted around the nation, 6,280 teenagers died in drunk-driving crashes.  In 1992 that number was down to 1,833.

# The Contract for Life

One of the most powerful tools that SADD has created is called the **Contract for Life.**  It reads as follows:

**Teenager:** I agree to call you for advice and/or transportation at any hour from any place if I am ever faced with a situation where a driver has been drinking or using illicit drugs.  I have discussed with you and fully understand your attitude toward any involvement with underage drinking or the use of illegal drugs.

**Parent:** I agree to come and get you at any hour, any place, no questions asked and no argument at that time, or I will pay for a taxi to bring you home safely.  I expect we would discuss this at a later time.

I agree to seek safe, sober transportation home if I am ever in a situation where I have had too much to drink or a friend who is driving me has had too much to drink.

Both parents and teenagers sign the contract.  Some people have criticized the program, arguing that parents who sign the pledge are condoning underage drinking.  But that's not always the case.  Even teens who don't drink may find themselves in a situation where their driver is drunk.  It may even be an adult, coming home drunk from a cocktail party and offering to drive a teenage baby-sitter home.

# CONTRACT FOR LIFE

## A Contract for Life
## Between Parents and Teenagers

Under this contract, we understand SADD encourages all youth to adopt a no use policy and obey the laws of their state with regards to alcohol and illicit drugs.

**Teenager**  I agree to call you for advice and/or transportation at any hour from any place if I am ever faced with a situation where a driver has been drinking or using illicit drugs. I have discussed with you and fully understand your attitude towards any involvement with underage drinking or the use of illegal drugs.

_____
Signature

**Parent**  I agree to come and get you at any hour, any place, no questions asked and no argument at that time, or I will pay for a taxi to bring you home safely. I expect we would discuss this at a later time.
I agree to seek safe, sober transportation home if I am ever in a situation where I have had too much to drink or a friend who is driving me has had too much to drink.

_____
Signature

_____
Date

Distributed by SADD, "Students Against Driving Drunk"

**Clearasil**    **Noxzema.**

**The contract for life requires that both teens and parents never drive drunk or ride with a person who has been drinking.**

Besides preventing drinking and driving, the Contract for Life also encourages communication between parents and teenagers. Sometimes parents just assume that their children know how adults feel and don't realize that families need to talk about the issues.

Sometimes kids feel awkward calling their parents in front of friends. SADD suggests that teens and parents come up with a code word for these situations. The teenager can pretend to call a friend, slip in the code word, and the parents will know that he or she is in an unsafe situation and needs a ride home. They can even agree to meet down the road a bit.

The other benefit of the Contract for Life is that it binds parents to the same rules. Many parents started driving when there were few restrictions on drinking and driving. The Contract for Life reminds parents of the new laws and attitudes towards DWI and shows that responsibility has to be a two-way street. And if parents want their teenagers to get home safely, they have to make sure they live up to their end of the bargain. They can't yell at their children when they pick them up at a party. And they themselves can't drink and drive.

"My father got into a DWI accident last month," says 17-year-old Mike Irving. "Fortunately, no one was hurt, but it made me so mad. It's always hard to resist peer pressure to drink, but I did it because it was part of the contract. My friends respected that. But now no one will believe me."

## How to Form a SADD Chapter
Sometimes students are the ones who want to form a SADD chapter; sometimes it's teachers and administrators. Either way works, but it's always a good idea to start talking about it well before the first meeting. People who want to start a chapter should begin to think about the issue. They can put up posters, send out flyers, and make announcements—get students' curiosity working. As many people as possible should become involved.

At the first meeting, you should decide what your chapter's goals will be. Then you can start working to meet those goals. Each SADD chapter tries to do what works best in its community. If the chapter needs help getting off the ground or building enthusiasm, speakers from the national office can come to the school and give a talk. Talk to your principal about setting aside a SADD day, when speakers and discussion groups on topics related to drinking and driving can bring the problems to your school's attention.

Above all, be careful not to criticize the students who

make the unwise decision to drink. You want them to listen to you so they will understand the danger and stop because they want to stay alive. If you make them mad by criticizing, they'll just tune you out.

## Other SADD Programs

The success of Students Against Driving Drunk has prompted other SADD spin-offs. In middle schools a nationwide SADD group has formed called Students Against Doing Drugs. It teaches about the dangers of drugs and alcohol and hopes to prevent their use.

Another group is called Student Athletes Detest Drugs. In this group's program, athletes sign a pledge to steer clear of drugs and alcohol, because "the use of those illegal substances . . . is destructive to a healthy lifestyle." They pledge to respect their mind and body and "continue with the best performance in both athletics and life."

Some schools make signing the pledge a requirement before students are allowed to participate in a sport. Breaking the pledge means being kicked off the team. One New Jersey high school takes the program a step further. It not only asks athletes not to use drugs and alcohol; it requires that these students stay away from parties where there might be drinking. Parents sign a pledge, too, supporting this program.

Alison Dill, a senior field hockey player, is frustrated with the school's new policy. "It would be really good if everyone was not drinking, but that's not the case. A lot of the parties still have drinking, so the athletes who really care about this suddenly have no social life. It's like we're being punished for being responsible. I think it would be better if we kept the pledge not to drink but were still allowed to go to parties."

# The Last Second

Robby Landry always knew he'd be a good driver. Speed limits were for other people. Robby knew he could maintain control even if he was going fast. "I'm a goalkeeper for my high school soccer team," Robby explains. "My reflexes are great, and tending goal keeps my eyes sharp. I always have to be looking for players out of the corners of my eyes, and that's what you do when you drive."

Webster Street is a straight, mile-long stretch of road not too far from Robby's home, where Robby was driving after drinking beer at a party. "I was going about 75, not even as fast as I've gone in the past," Robby recalls. "And I saw the car coming in the other direction, so I did ease up on the gas, just in case it was a cop."

All of a sudden a dog ran into the road in front of him. Robby slammed on the brakes, but he couldn't stop in time. "I was right about my good vision and reflexes, but it didn't matter. The car wasn't going to stop, no matter how quick I was on the brake."

The car skidded into the other lane, head on into the oncoming car. If Robby had had more experience or less to drink, he might have tried to swerve to the shoulder rather than try to stop. But that wasn't the case. The woman in the oncoming car tried to get out of the way, but there wasn't time. Robby's car slammed into her driver's side door and killed her on impact.

"Her death will be with me forever," says Robby. "I may even have to go to jail. I don't know yet. I do know that her three children no longer have a mother. It never occurred to me that I was risking someone else's life when I got behind the wheel after having a few beers. I thought it would be just me."

Alison thinks the program would get more support if it weren't so limiting. Because it's so restrictive, many student athletes just ignore it. Perhaps a less strict policy would encourage more followers. Schools have to find the right balance that would save the most lives.

## Safe Rides and Scared Stiff
While SADD is the largest student program to combat drinking and driving, there are others around the country that are also effective. One of these programs is called Safe Rides. Student drivers answer the phones at the Safe Rides hotline on Friday and Saturday nights. If a person is too drunk to drive but would rather not risk getting in trouble with his or her parents, the caller can ask Safe Rides for a ride instead. The program provides an alternative for those students who don't have good communication with their parents. It's also used by sober students who can't find a safe ride home.

Scared Stiff is a program started by a Maryland police officer named John DeVries. Seeing teenagers die because of drinking and driving was too much for DeVries, so he decided to do something about it. Scared Stiff is the result. DeVries says the program is "a 45-minute dose of reality." He has speakers and slides that illustrate the horror of DWI deaths, from the crash all the way to the morgue.

Programs like these are springing up all over the country as people are starting to notice how many teenagers are senselessly killed by drunk driving each year.

# WHAT YOU CAN DO

As groups like MADD and SADD have demonstrated, individuals can make a difference. If you want to cut down on DWI deaths, there are many things you can do.

**Be Responsible**    You can't convince others to change if you don't act responsibly yourself. Set a good example by never drinking if you're going to be driving. But if you find that you have had too much to drink, be responsible enough to give your car keys to a sober person, take a

---

### Did You Know...?

• People age 18-29 are the least likely to wear seat belts.

• Drunk Walking Isn't Safe, Either
Recent studies have shown that people who are drunk are nearly two times more likely than sober people to be killed just walking!

• Drivers with BACs above 0.15 were 380 times more likely than nondrinking drivers to be killed in a car crash.

taxi, or call someone to come pick you up.

But don't stop there. You may find yourself in a situation where the person driving you home has been drinking. If you're sober, try to convince that person to let you drive. If that isn't successful, or if you've been drinking, too, then just don't get in the car. It may make getting home more difficult, but at least you'll get there in one piece. Your actions may be enough to convince the driver to stop or to turn over the wheel to someone else. But even if you can't save his or her life, at least you will be saving your own.

If you're a host at a party, you have even more responsibility. It's no longer a matter of just wanting to protect your friends. You are now required by law to take their car keys away from them if they've had too much to drink. If you don't, you're considered just as responsible as they are for any crash they get into that night. If there are victims in the crash and they want to sue you, they will most likely win.

When you are a host, make sure you have plenty of food available. People get drunk quicker on an empty stomach. Make sure there are plenty of nonalcoholic alternatives. And most important, keep a careful watch on who is driving.

## Protect Yourself

The sad truth about drinking and driving is that a careful, sober person can still wind up as the victim of someone else. In fact, every year, approximately 1.64 million innocent people will be hurt or killed in a drunk-driving crash.

So you have to learn to protect yourself from the actions of irresponsible drivers, and the best thing you can do is to

Students Against Drunk Driving (SADD) spreads awareness about DWI. These students have painted their faces white to signify the death of a person every 22-24 minutes.

buckle up. Make sure you and everyone in your car are wearing seat belts. At least you will have reduced your risk of dying if you do end up in a crash. Studies have shown that if you wear a seat belt, you can cut your risk in half.

Driving defensively helps, too, especially if you're out late at night. The National Highway Traffic Safety Administration reports that there are eight times as many alcohol-related car crashes at night than during the day.

## Take Action

One of the best things you can do to cut down on DWI is to educate others about the dangers of drinking and driving. Get into discussions with your friends. Tell them what you know. You can influence people you don't know by writing letters to the newspaper. Write to members of Congress and of state legislatures and express your desire to have stronger drunk-driving laws passed.

On a more personal level, you can get involved in SADD or Safe Rides. If your school doesn't have a chapter, you can start one. Talk about it with your friends. Get parents and teachers involved, too. The more people who are aware of the hazards of DWI, the safer our roads will be.

And if you ever see a drunk driver on the road, get the car's license plate number and call the police immediately. You may be saving someone's life.

# FOR MORE
# INFORMATION

Mothers Against Drunk Driving (MADD)
P.O. Box 541688
Dallas, TX  75354-1688
(214) 744-6233

National Commission Against Drunk Driving
1900 L Street NW, Suite 705
Washington, DC  20036
(202) 452-6004

National Highway Traffic Safety Administration
400 7th Street SW
Washington, DC  20590
(202) 366-9550

Students Against Driving Drunk (SADD)
P.O. Box 800
Marlboro, MA  01752
(508) 481-3568

# GLOSSARY/ INDEX

**ADMINISTRATIVE LICENSE REVOCATION (ALR)**—*15–16* A program in more than half the states that allows police officers to remove a drunk driver's license at the scene of the arrest.

**BLOOD ALCOHOL CONTENT (BAC)**—*9–10* The official measure of the amount of alcohol in the body. It is illegal for a driver's BAC to be over 0.08 in some states, 0.10 in others. Some states have a lower BAC for people under 21.

**BREATHALYZER**—*10* A machine that measures a person's BAC from a breath sample.

**COMMUNITY SERVICE**—*13* A sentence often given to first-time DWI offenders. They must spend a certain number of hours doing volunteer work in their community.

**CONTRACT FOR LIFE**—*35* A pledge that both parents and teenagers sign to prevent them from being victims of DWI.

**DESIGNATED DRIVER**—*18* A person chosen in advance not to drink. That person will later drive a group of people home.

**DRIVING UNDER THE INFLUENCE (DUI)**—*6–7* The practice of driving while under the influence of alcohol or other drugs.

**DRIVING WHILE INTOXICATED (DWI)**—*6*   The practice of driving when intoxicated or impaired.

**INTOXICATED**—*6*   Having a BAC above 0.10, or 0.08 in some states.

**LICENSE REVOCATION**—*13*   A penalty that takes away a driver's license for a certain period of time. At the end of the period, the offender must reapply for a new license.

**LICENSE SUSPENSION**—*13*   A penalty that takes away a driver's license for a certain period of time and then returns it when the time is over.

**LOBBY**—*25*   To put arguments and pressure before government officials in an effort to convince them to vote a certain way.

**MOTHERS AGAINST DRUNK DRIVING (MADD)**—*25*   A group whose goal is to make the country aware that drunk driving is a crime.

**SAFE RIDES**—*40*   A program that provides rides to young people who are intoxicated and cannot drive themselves or who are at risk of driving with someone who is intoxicated.

**SOBRIETY CHECKPOINTS**—*16*   The stopping of all vehicles on a certain segment of road to check for drunk or impaired drivers.

**STANDARDIZED FIELD SOBRIETY TESTS**—*11*   The tasks that a police officer will request of a suspected DWI offender. The results usually indicate whether the driver should be arrested.

**STUDENTS AGAINST DRUNK DRIVING (SADD)**—*34* A group geared toward teenagers that teaches the dangers of drinking and driving and stresses self-reliance when deciding not to do it.

**VICTIM IMPACT PANEL**—*21* A group of victims of DWI crashes who tell their stories to DWI offenders.

**20 x 2,000 PROGRAM**—*26* A Mothers Against Drunk Driving (MADD) campaign to reduce DWI deaths by 20 percent by the year 2000.